JOHANN STRAUSS

Die Fledermaus

ENGLISH VERSION
by
RUTH and THOMAS MARTIN

Ed. 2024

G. SCHIRMER, Inc.

DISTRIBUTED BY
HAL•LEONARD®
CORPORATION
7777 W. BLUEMOUND RD. P.O. BOX 13819 MILWAUKEE, WI 53213

Act II

No. 6.   Entr'acte and Chorus

-ca-sion. So u-nique, so de-light ful, it's the par-ty of the year!

-ca-sion. So u-nique, so de-light ful, it's the par-ty of the year!

-ca-sion. So u-nique, so de-light ful, it's the par-ty of the year!

Nothing could be more in-triguing than this most en-chanting at-mosphere.

Nothing could be more in-triguing than this most en-chanting at-mosphere.

most en-chanting at-mosphere.

Let us all be hap-py while we may, we still are young and gay.   For to-

Let us all be hap-py while we may, we still are young and gay.

we are young and gay.

No. 8. Ensemble and Couplets

Adele, Orlofsky, Eisenstein, Falke, and Chorus

Un poco meno mosso

ORLOFSKY:
See this de-light-ful la-dy, Marquis Re-nard takes her for .. no, I can't be-lieve it .. For what then? Take a guess!

4 SOPRANOS

FALKE
He takes me for a chambermaid on hol-i-day par-ade.

ADELE

Più animato

ORLOFSKY WITH SOPRANOS
Ha ha ha ha ha ha ha

TUTTI FALKE WITH TENOR II
Ha ha ha ha

Più animato
Ha ha ha ha

ha ha ha,
cresc.
ha, He's try-ing to be fun-ny, ha ha ha ha ha, ha ha!

cresc.
ha ha, He's try-ing to be fun-ny, ha ha ha ha ha ha ha!

cresc.
ha ha, He's try-ing to be fun-ny, ha ha ha ha ha ha ha!

cresc.

ril.

Meno

ORLOFSKY

Mar - quis, you are most im - po - lite, you sure - ly are mistaken! How im-po-

- lite!

FALKE   EISENSTEIN

How im - po - lite!   The like - ness was a shock to me!

How im - po - lite!

TUTTI

How im - po - lite!   How im - po -

How im - po - lite!   How im - po -

grazioso

EISENSTEIN

I could have sworn that it was she!

How im - po - lite!

- lite!

- lite!

rit.

Allegretto
ADELE

1. My dear Marquis, it seems to me you should dis-play more tact! _____
2. Just look at me and you will see there's more than meets the eye . _____

Allegretto

_____ Where a la-dy goes, what a la-dy shows, is how she
_____ Where a la-dy's been, where a la-dy's seen, are proofs that

proves the fact! My taste is too fine and too chic, ah_____ My
nev-er lie. Could I be at home in this room, ah_____ If

waist has a line too u-nique, ah. _____ My talk is too dra-ma-tic, my
I were at home with a broom, ah. _____ The way I lift an eye-brow is

walk a - ris - to - crat-ic. What chambermaid you know could have so much to show, what
ty - pic - al - ly highbrow! what chambermaid you know could have so much to show, what

cham - bermaid you know could have so much to show? In-stead of put - ting
cham - bermaid you know could have so much to show? You might as well ad -

on such airs, why don't you mind your own af - fairs? It's too fun - ny, ha ha ha,
- mit, Mar - quis, you owe me an a - pol - o - gy. It's too fun - ny, ha ha ha,

Please excuse me, ha ha ha, I can't help it, ha ha ha, You amuse me, ha ha ha ha ha ha.
Please excuse me, ha ha ha, I can't help it, ha ha ha, You amuse me, ha ha ha ha haha.

ADELE

It's too fun - ny, ha ha ha, Please ex - cuse me, ha ha ha ha, _____

CHORUS

It's too fun - ny, ha ha ha, Please ex - cuse me, ha ha ha ha ha ha

It's too fun - ny, ha ha ha, Please ex - cuse me, ha ha ha ha ha ha

It's too fun - ny, ha ha ha, Please ex - cuse me, ha ha ha ha ha ha.

ha ___ ha, __ You're wrong as you can be, Mar -

ha ha ha ha ha ha ha!

ha ha ha ha ha ha ha!

ha ha ha ha ha ha ha!

quis

No. 11. Finale of Act II

Principals and Chorus

EISENSTEIN: . . . *A toast to the life of our party, — to King Champagne!*

ORLOFSKY
1. Champagne's de - li - cious bub - bles, tra -

EISENSTEIN.
2. pagne is — so ma - jes - tic, tra -

ADELE
3. pagne is — so ro - man - tic, tra -

PIANO

la la la la la la la, scat - ter all our troub - les tra - la la la la la

la la la la la la la, for - eign and do - mes - tic, tra - la la la la la

la la la la la la la, glo - rious and gi - gan - tic, tra - la la la la la

O. 1. la.— It mel - lows pol - i - ti - cians and bet - ters world con - di - tions. All

E. 2. la.— It makes the world we live in, a bet - ter place to give in! All

A. 3. la.— It makes the world look thrill - ing, and men be - come more will - ing! All

see that hap - py couples are meeting, that many hearts with true love are beating; So

why not con - ti - nue in this hap - py mood and sing to love and bro - ther-

rit.

ORLOFSKY

- hood! I a - gree most heart - i - ly, that's good. Let us sing to love and bro - ther-

CHORUS

Let us sing to love and bro - ther-

Let us sing to love and bro - ther-

EISENSTEIN (to Rosal.)

ROSALINDA

-hood! You, too, love - ly la - dy, must be there. When all are kiss- ing, I

-hood!

- hood!

FALKE

can't be missing. Let's lift our glas-ses and drink a-gain, and ev - 'ry-bod-y

join the refrain.

Allegretto moderato

Sing to love, __ love we nev-er knew be-fore, __

__ May it flourish and bloom for ev - er-more, Sing to love, __ ev-erlast - ing

hap-pi-ness, let us all — be friends to-geth - er. —— For e-

-ter - ni - ty, a fra - ter - ni - ty of com - pan - ions,

friends, and lov - ers. _____ First a kiss,

then one more, you, you, and al - ways you! _

_ You kiss me, I kiss you, you,

you, on - ly you, on - ly you, on - ly, on - ly

Tempo I (Allegretto moderato)

ORLOFSKY: Sing to love, __ love we nev-er knew be-fore, __ May it flour- ish and

EISENSTEIN: Sing to love, __ love we nev - er knew be-fore, __

FALKE: you!

FALKE, FRANK: Sing to love, __

Tempo I. (Allegretto moderato.)

mf

ROSALINDA-WITH SOPRANO: Sing to love, __ love we nev - er knew be-fore,

ADELE, SALLY: Sing to love, __

ORLOFSKY: bloom for ev - er - more. Let us __

EISENSTEIN: May it flour- ish for ev - er - more,

FALKE, FRANK: __ love we nev-er knew be-fore, __ May it flour- ish for

26

30

la la la _____ la la!

la la la _____ la la!

la la la _____ la la!

la la la _____ la la!

la la la _____ la la!

la la la _____ la la!

la la la _____ la la!

la la la _____ la la!

la la la _____ la la!

la la _____ la la!

la la _____ la la!

Tempo di Polka

SOPR.
ALT.

CHORUS

TEN.
BASS

Come on, my darling, dance with me and

Tempo di Polka

(Bohemian)

trip the Pol - ka mer -ri- ly, while fiddlers gaily bow the strings, and ev - 'ry-body

laughs and sings. Come on, my dar - ling, dance with me and trip the Pol - ka

mer - ri - ly, while fid -dlers gaily bow the strings, and ev -'ry -body laughs and sings

Take your partner by the hand, stamp-ing, hop-ping, nev-er stopping. There's no better

mu-sic band an-y-where in all the land! Come

on, my dar-ling, dance with me and trip the Pol-ka mer-ri-ly, while fid-dlers gai-ly

bow the strings, and ev'ry-bod-y laughs and sings! Come on my darling dance with me and

trip the Pol - ka   mer - ri - ly, while fid - dlers gai - ly   bow the strings, and

ev - 'ry - bod y laughs and sings!

Allegro maestoso

(Hungarian)

ALL SOLOISTS AND CHORUS

sit - u - a-tion.   Ah, happy day of divine de-

sit - u - a - tion.   Ah, happy day of divine de-

sit - u - a - tion.   Ah, happy day of divine de-

cresc.

- light! Love and champagne banish care from sight. Could we live on as we

- light! Love and champagne banish care from sight. Could we live on as we

- light! Love and champagne banish care from sight. Could we live on as we

do to - night,   life would for - ev - er be gay and bright.

do to - night,   life would for - ev - er be gay and bright.

do to - night,   life would for - ev - er be gay and bright.

40

(drawing him forward confidentially)

ROSALINDA

My friend, do not ask what I con-ceal, the shock you would get would make you reel.

ADELE, ORLOFSKY, AND SALLY

Ha ha ha ha, she is no fool, in-deed, she's no-bo-dy's fool!

EISENSTEIN

Hu hu hu hu, you are too cruel, you are too cruel.

ADELE

Are you a-

SOLOISTS AND CHORUS

In-deed, she's no-bo-dy's fool!

In-deed, she's no-bo-dy's fool!

she's no-bo-dy's fool!

Più mosso

EISENSTEIN (startled)

FRANK (also)

six. Where's my hat? Where's my coat? It is very late, Where's my hat? Where's my coat? It is

Più mosso.

very late.

SOLOISTS AND CHORUS

They are looking for

Bring his hat, bring his coat, O don't make him wait!

Bring his hat, bring his coat, O don't make him wait!

Bring his hat, bring his coat, O don't make him wait!

FRANK

FRANK, EISENSTEIN

me! And I know where I should be! Where's my hat? Where's my coat? O give me my

(Servants bring various coats and hats which do not fit)

coat! *acceler.*

Bring his coat, bring his hat, bring his coat, ha ha ha, bring his hat, O bring him his

Bring his coat, bring his hat, bring his coat, ha ha ha, bring his hat, O bring him his

Bring his coat, bring his hat, bring his coat, ha ha ha, bring his hat, O bring him his

FRANK (leaning on Eisenstein)   EISENSTEIN

Dear Mar - quis,   I   hope you will call   on me. Yes, in-

coat, ha ha ha!

coat, ha ha ha!

coat, ha ha ha!

ADELE. SALLY

ORLOFSKY   Good - bye, good- bye, ha ha!
FALKE
Good - bye, good- bye, ha ha!

EISENSTEIN   EISENSTEIN; FRANK

-deed, the moment my time is free.   Let's say good - bye.

la—— la—— la la la —— la la la!

bright, then life would be for - ev — er gay and bright.

bright, then life would be for - ev — er gay and bright.

bright, then life would be for - ev — er gay and bright.

(Eisenstein and Frank, dancing the last tempo, move, staggering, arm in arm toward the background.

They are surrounded by the dancers, while the curtain falls.)

End of Act II

47

No. 16.   Finale of Act III
Full Company

TUTTI

braggart with his master wit has fal-len in the pit.

braggart with his master wit has fal-len in the pit. **EISENSTEIN** Won't you tell me out and

braggart with his master wit has fal-len in the pit.

FALKE

out what is this sto-ry all a-bout? And what are you driving at? It's the

FALKE

ven-geance of the Bat! Yes, the vengeance of the Bat!

Yes, the vengeance of the Bat! But _____ the

TUTTI Yes, the vengeance of the Bat! But _____ the

Yes, the vengeance of the Bat! But _____ the

joke you played with such a bang turned out to be a boom-e-rang. This time it was the

joke you played with such a bang turned out to be a boom-e-rang. This time it was the

joke you played with such a bang turned out to be a boom-e-rang. This time it was the

clev-er Bat who gave you tit for tat!

EISENSTEIN

clev-er Bat who gave you tit for tat!

Do explain it

clev-er Bat who gave you tit for tat!

FALKE

from the start. All the an-guish you went through, was a joke I played on

50

End of Operetta